THIRTEEN
COLONIAL
AMERICANA

THIRTEEN
COLONIAL
AMERICANA

A selection of publications
issued in the British Provinces
of North America during
the final half-century
of the Colonial era

Edited by Edward Connery Lathem

WASHINGTON, D. C.
Association of Research Libraries
1977

This publication was made possible
through a grant from
THE COMMONWEALTH FUND

INTRODUCTORY NOTE

The works featured herein have been chosen to represent something of the nature and variety of products of the American press during the years 1727 through 1776—as the thirteen Provinces moved toward the severing of their Colonial ties and a declaration of their political independence. One item has been chosen for each Colony. Arrangement is chronological by date of publication.

PREFATORY SUBSCRIPTION

Our country having marked its Bicentennial and now being entered upon its third century, we, the undersigned, on behalf of those States which translated themselves from Colonies of Great Britain into the thirteen originating United States of America, warmly join in this tribute to the Colonial heritage from which publishing emerged and has developed within the American republic.

ELLA GRASSO
Governor of Connecticut

BRENDAN BYRNE
Governor of New Jersey

PIERRE S. DUPONT
Governor of Delaware

HUGH L. CAREY
Governor of New York

GEORGE BUSBEE
Governor of Georgia

JAMES B. HUNT JR.
Governor of North Carolina

BLAIR LEE III
Acting Governor of Maryland

MILTON J. SHAPP
Governor of Pennsylvania

MICHAEL S. DUKAKIS
Governor of Massachusetts

J. JOSEPH GARRAHY
Governor of Rhode Island

MELDRIM THOMSON JR.
Governor of New Hampshire

JAMES B. EDWARDS
Governor of South Carolina

MILLS E. GODWIN JR.
Governor of Virginia

THIRTEEN
COLONIAL
AMERICANA

I

Massachusetts

Cotton Mather

Christian Loyalty

1727

Chriſtian LOYALTY.

OR,

Some Suitable Sentiments

On the WITHDRAW of

King *GEORGE* the Firſt,

Of Glorious Memory,

And the ACCESS of

King *GEORGE* the Second,

Unto the Throne of the

BRITISH EMPIRE.

By *Cotton Mather*, D. D.
and F. R. S.

———*Uno avulſo non deficit Alter Aureus*———

BOSTON:

Printed and Sold by *T. Fleet*, at his Print-
ing-Houſe in *Pudding-Lane*, near the
Town-Houſe, 1727.

I. *Massachusetts*

WRITING in 1827, one hundred years after Cotton Mather's death, the historian Thomas Carlyle defined the three great elements of modern civilization as gunpowder, printing, and the Protestant religion. This attitude, of course, had its origin in English history, in which printing and the Protestant religion were especially intertwined. Nowhere is this more clearly seen than in the religious state of 17th- and 18th-Century New England.

As early as 1638, only eighteen years after the settlement in Plymouth, an Englishman, the Rev. Jose Glover, prepared to introduce printing into North America by establishing a press in Cambridge, Massachusetts. To accompany him, he chose a locksmith, Stephen Daye, who is now known as North America's first printer. The minister was never to see his press established, for he died during the voyage to the new world, and it was left to his wife to install the press on the grounds of Harvard College. The direction of the press was entrusted to Henry Dunster, the first president of Harvard College, who later married Mrs. Glover, but the actual work of printing was conducted by Stephen Daye. Daye was neither an educated man nor a printer, and the first products of the press suffered, accordingly, from poor workmanship and typographical errors. The achievement, despite primitive conditions in a small candle-lit shop, was nevertheless magnificent.

Among the first products of the press at Cambridge was "The Bay Psalm Book." While "The Bay Psalm Book" is important in the history of American printing, it symbolizes, moreover, the dominant role of religion in New England society. It was primarily a psalmbook, a prayer book for the general population, but it was also a translation of the Psalms from the Hebrew into a metrical English by Colonial clergymen. This was an amazing feat of erudition for such a relatively small society, and it indicates something of the role which the ministers, the real rulers of this theocratic state, played and the reason they were able to play it. The Protestant divines were an aristocracy of the intellect, who dominated the population by the force of their character and their scholarship. They exercised an influence over the whole fabric of society in a variety of ways, but particularly from the pulpit—and that extension of the pulpit, the printed sermon, which accounted for a very large portion of the output of the New England Colonial presses.

Perhaps the epitome of the Protestant divine was Cotton Mather. He was a third generation minister. Both his grandfathers, John Cotton and Richard Mather, had contributed to "The Bay Psalm Book." Increase Mather, his father, was a towering figure in his own right, and while he always remained a minister of the gospel, he was also a significant figure in politics, playing a role on both sides of the Atlantic (so much so, that in 1692 he was given the royal favor of nominating the Governor of Massachusetts and his principal officers). Increase Mather's scholarship led him to friendships with renowned scholars of his time, such as the scientist Richard Boyle. His output of printed works was extensive; about one hundred and thirty books or pamphlets are attributed to him alone (among them was the first book printed in Boston, *The Wicked Mans Portion*, which appeared in 1676).

His son, Cotton Mather (1662–1727), appeared both to some of his contemporaries and to later readers as intolerant, stern, unlovable, opinionated, casuistic to the point of hypocrisy, and ill-tempered. He did not possess the direct influence his father enjoyed on the government of the Commonwealth, nor was he able to succeed his father as president of Harvard, despite his scholarly attainments and family position. (He even complained that for him to advocate a position was enough for others to oppose it.) Yet, he was a man of prodigious energy and enormous intellectual prowess, dedicated to the service of God as he perceived it. Throughout his life he busied himself with "good causes" of every kind: the building of churches, the relief of needy ministers, Indian missions, and so forth. He poured out his thought in a stream of correspondence and in more than four hundred and fifty books on a wide variety of subjects, including history and science, as well as religion. His fame as a scholar was widespread, at home and abroad. Glasgow University acknowledged it by making him a Doctor of Divinity in 1710 and the Royal Society by making him a Fellow in 1713. He had innumerable distinguished correspondents and immense social influence, and he was a constantly quoted author and a much-sought-after preacher.

Christian Loyalty, published by Cotton Mather in the last year of his life, is a minor work that does not bear comparison with his more important *Magnalia Christi Americana; or, The Ecclesiastical History of New-England, from Its First Planting* ... (1702) or with his *Bonifacius* (1710) which was praised by Benjamin Franklin and widely read at the time. But *Christian Loyalty* is representative of the kind of published sermon that was so important in New England. It expresses the devotion of the Mather family to the House of Hanover, which was identified with the preservation of the Protestant order, in opposition to the Papist pretensions of James II and the heirs of the House of Stuart. The sermon is typical of the preacher's use of a secular event to embroider a religious theme and to link a political fact with religious fidelity.

Christian Loyalty also marks the passing of one reign and the beginning of another, the death of George I and the accession of George II—pre-figuring, in an unintended sense, the future severing of some of the bonds with the mother country. Written, as it was, at the end of Mather's life, it foreshadows, too, the passing of an era, the decline of Puritanism and an increase in tolerance. It is particularly appropriate as the first of a selection of works representing publishing in America during the final half-century of the Colonial era.

RICHARD J. TALBOT
Director of Libraries,
University of Massachusetts

II

Rhode Island

Rhode Island Colony

Acts and Laws

1730

ACTS

AND

LAWS,

Of His Majesty's

COLONY

OF

Rhode-Island,

AND

Providence-Plantations,
In *AMERICA*.

NEWPORT, *Rhode-Island* :
Printed by J AMES F RANKLIN, and Sold at his Shop near
the Town School-House. 1730.

slightly
reduced

II. *Rhode Island*

THE earliest settlers of British North America found scant need for the printer. Although word of mouth and oral proclamations supplied a satisfactory means of disseminating news, the London printing houses provided what legal, literary, or religious work needed to be done. Resorting to printers overseas (or, alternatively, to ones in other Colonies) soon proved slow and cumbersome, especially for the Colonial Governors and legislatures needing to publish promptly a variety of acts, laws, and regulations. The establishment of printing presses was, accordingly, a response to a need, and this was indeed true in His Majesty's Colony of Rhode-Island and Providence-Plantations.

In a short time, business generated by Colonial authorities became the bread-and-butter work of the earliest printing houses. The printer received, thus, a fairly dependable basic income, while he sought other work that was additionally profitable. Government printing, newspapers, almanacs, currency, and blank forms became the staple commodity of the Colonial printer, because they were essential to daily life. The issuance of creative works had to wait until the frontier was controlled, and until there was leisure for contemplating things of the mind.

If America's infant printing industry was grateful to the Colonial governments, the reverse was also true; many authorities welcomed the opportunity, provided by the existence of printing houses, to codify and disseminate their bodies of laws and regulations. It was, however, three years from the advent, in 1727, of a printer in Rhode Island before the Assembly took advantage of his presence to issue *Acts and Laws, of His Majesty's Colony of Rhode-Island, and Providence-Plantations, in America.*

For an example of pioneer printing, this volume is a substantial work. *Acts and Laws* is bound with *The Charter Granted by His Majesty King Charles The Second, to the Colony of Rhode-Island, and Providence-Plantations, in America.* Each work has its own title page and pagination. Eleven years earlier the General Assembly had gone to Boston for the first printing of the laws of the Colony. Here, for the first time, the royal charter of 1663 and the laws were printed within the Colony itself.

The layout of the title page is balanced and formal, resembling in style what prevailed in England. It is adorned with a magnificent woodcut of the arms of the Colony, consisting of a shield bearing an anchor, with the motto "HOPE" above, and the whole surrounded by an ornamental design.

As with many such documents, the volume affords the modern reader a glimpse of manners, customs, and attitudes of life in the Colonial period. Here one may find the resolutions and texts of the governing laws, beginning with those passed by the General Assembly in 1663. While the first official act of this Assembly was one of a housekeeping nature, regulating the election of general officers, the two which follow demonstrate a concern for the welfare of the citizenry and the indigenous population: "An Act for Declaring the Rights and Priviledges of His Majesties Subjects within this Colony" and "An Act for the Preventing of Illegal and Clandestine Purchases of the Native Indians in this Colony."

Also included in the *Acts and Laws* are regulations of courts, ferries, fishermen, fence-keepers, slaves, highways, and currency—and for the prevention of drunkenness and counterfeiting. Reimbursement for mileage costs, for example, is hardly a modern practice, for under "Sheriff's Fees" we note, "For all Executions Served out of the Town where the Sheriff Lives, *Two pence per* Mile, forward and backward." "Executions" no doubt referred to common legal transactions, but under "Attorney General's Fees" one pound sterling was paid "For every Criminal Executed to Death."

The first printer in Rhode Island was James Franklin (1697–1735), who established his press in Newport in 1727. Franklin is perhaps best known as the harsh, ill-mannered master depicted by his younger brother and apprentice, Benjamin, in the latter's *Autobiography*. Indeed, the great statesman credited James with one of the clues to his greatness: "I fancy his harsh and tyrannical treatment of me might be a means of impressing me with that aversion to arbitrary power that has stuck to me through my whole life."

James Franklin had set up his first press in Boston in 1717, having learned his trade in London. He was for two years printer of William Brooker's *Boston Gazette*, and in 1721 he launched the *New-England Courant*, a newspaper whose witty and satirical assaults on the Boston establishment earned him a month in prison and a prohibition from publishing the paper. He finally quit Boston and, with the promise of his becoming public printer there, moved to Rhode Island. He founded that Colony's first newspaper, the *Rhode-Island Gazette*, during 1732. His wife, Anne, and son, James, carried on the business after his death in 1735, it being the only printing house in the Colony until 1762.

The *Acts and Laws* of 1730 is a significant example of printing emanating from Rhode Island's first press. It gave the printer a position of respect in the life of the Colony; it disseminated in an orderly manner the work of the government; and it provided a safeguard to the people's liberties.

CHARLES CHURCHWELL
University Librarian,
Brown University

III

New York

John Peter Zenger

A Brief Narrative of the Case and Tryal

1736

A brief Narrative of the Case and Try-al of *John Peter Zenger*, Printer of the *New-York weekly Journal*.

A S There was but one Printer in the Province of *New-York*, that printed a publick News Paper, I was in Hopes, if I undertook to pub-lish another, I might make it worth my while ; and I soon found my Hopes were not groundless: My first Paper was printed, *Nov. 5th,* 1733. and I continued printing and publishing of them, I thought to the Satisfaction of every Body, till the *January* following; when the Chief Justice was pleased to animadvert upon the Doctrine of Libels, in a long Charge given in that Term to the Grand Jury, and afterwards on the third *Tuesday* of *October,* 1734. was again pleased to charge the Grand Jury in the following Words.

' *Gentlemen* ; I shall conclude with reading a Paragraph or two out of the
' same Book, concerning Libels ; they are arrived to that Height, that they
' call loudly for your Animadversion ; it is high Time to put a Stop to them ;
' for at the rate Things are now carried on, when all Order and Government
' is endeavoured to be trampled on ; Reflections are cast upon Persons of all
' Degrees, must not these Things end in Sedition, if not timely prevented ? Lenity,
' you have seen will not avail, it becomes you then to enquire after the Of-
' fenders, that we may in a due Course of Law be enabled to punish them.
' If you, *Gentlemen,* do not interpose, consider whether the ill Consequences
' that may arise from any Disturbances of the publick Peace, may not in part,
' lye at your Door ?
' *Hawkins,* in his Chapter of Libels, considers three Points. 1*st. What shall*
' *be said to be a Libel.* 2*dly. Who are lyable to be punished for it.* 3*dly. In what*
' *Manner they are to be punished.* Under the 1*st.* he says, §. 7. *Nor can there be*
' *any Doubt, but that a Writing which defames a private Person only, is as much*
' *a Libel as that which defames Persons intrusted in a publick Capacity, in as much*
' *as it manifestly tends to create ill Blood, and to cause a Disturbance of the publick Peace;*
' *however, it is certain, that it is a very high Aggravation of a Libel, that it tends to*
' *scandalize the Government, by reflecting on those who are entrusted with the Admini-*
' *stration of publick Affairs, which does not only endanger the publick Peace, as all other*
' *Libels do, by stirring up the Parties immediately concerned in it, to Acts of Revenge,*
' *but also has a direct Tendency to breed in the People a Dislike of their Governours,*
' *and incline them to Faction and Sedition.* As to the 2*d.* Point he says, §. 10.
' *It is certain, not only he who composes or procures another to compose it, but*
' *also that he who publishes, or procures another to publish it, are in Danger of being*
' *punished for it ; and it is said not to be material whether he who disperses a Libel,*
' *knew any Thing of the Contents or Effects of it or not ; for nothing could be more*

A   *easy*

slightly reduced

III. *New York*

THE facts concerning the trial of John Peter Zenger have been fully and carefully set forth many times, most recently by Stanley Nider Katz in his introduction to a 1963 edition of *A Brief Narrative*. Zenger, who came to New York as an immigrant at age thirteen, learned the printing trade as an apprentice to William Bradford, the public printer of the Province of New York, and in 1726 set up his own shop. His fame—and, in a real sense, his troubles—began with the first issue of the *New-York Weekly Journal*, which came from Zenger's press in November of 1733. From the beginning, the *Journal* (one of less than a dozen newspapers then published in the American Colonies) was in large part the voice of James Alexander and others who had rallied to the support of Lewis Morris, a prominent and powerful New Yorker dismissed as Chief Justice of the Supreme Court by the Crown's poorly regarded Governor, William Cosby. In issue after issue of the paper, through satire, critical discussions of government policy, and direct attack on the Governor and those sharing in his spoils, the pages of the *Journal* made the case against Cosby and promoted the already-popular cause of Morris.

To stem the growing tide of opposition, Cosby had offending issues of the *Journal* burned and Zenger arrested for "printing and publishing several seditious libels . . . tending to raise factions and tumults among the people of this Province, inflaming their minds with contempt of His Majesty's government, and greatly disturbing the peace thereof. . . ."

Five days after Zenger's imprisonment, leading lawyers supporting the Morris cause urged that low bail be set and the printer freed. Instead, Chief Justice De Lancey fixed bail at four hundred pounds, and Zenger, unable to raise such an unprecedented sum, spent the next eight months in cramped quarters in the attic jail of City Hall. Legal and extralegal maneuverings by Cosby and his appointees on the bench aroused pro-Zenger sympathies and, ultimately, led to the disbarment of Zenger's lawyers, when they chose to test the validity of the commissions of the judges themselves. This last action set the stage for the entrance of Andrew Hamilton, a lawyer of exceptional skill and perception, who had been brought from Philadelphia to assist in Zenger's defense.

At the heart of the case against Zenger was the law of seditious libel, established and refined in Star Chamber proceedings more than a century earlier. In essence, the law held that published statements critical of officials or the institutions of government were a valid basis for prosecution for libel, regardless of whether those statements were true or false, simply because such criticism tended to bring government into disrepute.

With clear purpose, Hamilton's defense of Zenger ignored the law and urged the jury to consider whether truth itself was not a sufficient and appropriate defense against a charge of libel. His powerful arguments concerning freedom of expression and the right and obligation of juries to stand as bulwarks against neglect of the law and abuses by magistrates were articulate and effective, and despite a final admonishment by the Chief Justice to limit the scope of their deliberations, the jury reached a not-guilty verdict, after deliberating only a few minutes.

Zenger was released and he returned to his press. In a few years' time he succeeded to the post of public printer, and the *New-York Weekly Journal* continued until 1751, published, following Zenger's death in 1746, by his wife and, finally, by a son.

A Brief Narrative, the detailed account of the trial, first published in 1736, is judged to be the work of James Alexander, who probably drew on notes prepared by Andrew Hamilton. The work occasionally figured in other libel cases, and it was republished a number of times in England, as well as in New York and Boston, before the end of the 18th Century. Recently, historians have diverted from 19th-Century assertions that the Zenger trial was a fundamental turning point in establishing a free press in America and in transforming legal perceptions of libel. Revision of the law did, in fact, require several legislative acts, in both England and post-Revolutionary America. The Zenger case was and is important, however, because for more than two centuries it has underscored, in the minds of Americans, the fact that in a republic the concerns of the populace must, in the end, mold the law.

A plaque on the wall of St. Paul's Protestant Episcopal Church, located in an old and now-dreary section of Mount Vernon, New York, only a block or two from the New York City line, notes that the site was once the "ancient village green of Eastchester, a general training ground and election place in Colonial days and enlisting headquarters for Revolutionary soldiers." In 1733, an election held on the Eastchester Green was flawed by efforts of the sheriff and other officials to keep supporters of Lewis Morris (and, hence, opponents of Governor Cosby) from casting their votes. This obvious attempt at intimidation was reported by Zenger in his *Weekly Journal*, serving to arouse the wrath of Cosby and stimulating the subsequent efforts to stop publication of the newspaper.

Close by St. Paul's Church an historical marker calls attention to that election and the resulting Zenger trial. (Similar markers spread across the country, often in equally unlikely places, symbolize other events—and, cumulatively, our history.) Given the changing interpretations by historians, perhaps the trial is today best seen as an event which, when joined with others before and after, helped clarify the substance of an issue of immense importance. Like the marker in Mount Vernon, the trial of John Peter Zenger reminds us of a distant time and occasion when a fundamental question was posed and answered. Individually and together, we are in need of such touchstones to keep us on course. In this sense, *A Brief Narrative of the Case and Tryal of John Peter Zenger* is a Colonial document of great importance.

WARREN J. HAAS
Vice President and University Librarian,
Columbia University

IV

Virginia

William Stith

*The History of the First Discovery
and Settlement of Virginia*

1747

THE

HISTORY

OF THE

First DISCOVERY

AND

SETTLEMENT

OF

VIRGINIA:

BEING

An ESSAY towards a General
HISTORY of this COLONY.

By WILLIAM STITH. *A. M.*
Rector of *Henrico* Parish, and one of the Governors of
William and *Mary* COLLEGE.

Tantæ molis erat *** *condere gentem.*   Virg.

WILLIAMSBURG:
Printed by WILLIAM PARKS, M,DCC,XLVII.

IV. *Virginia*

THE Rev. William Stith (1707–1755) was born in Virginia, educated at the William & Mary Grammar School and at Queen's College, Oxford, became rector of Henrico Parish in Virginia, and in 1752 was appointed the third president of the College of William & Mary. He began his *History of the First Discovery and Settlement of Virginia* sometime after 1732 at Henrico Parish, acting on a fear that "many useful Papers and Records, relating to our History . . . will perhaps be lost hereafter" and realizing "how empty and unsatisfactory every thing, yet published upon the Subject, is." Stith was also motivated by a sense of the unjust treatment of Englishmen in the Colony by the Crown, and the toast he drank against a fee leveled by Governor Dinwiddie on each patent for land became well known throughout Virginia: "Liberty & Property and no Pistole."

Stith's portrait of King James I, whom he considered arbitrary and unjust, appears in his "Preface" to the *History* and is worth quoting: "For he had been bred up under *Buchanan*, one of the brightest Genius's and most accomplished Scholars of that Age, who had given him *Greek* and *Latin* in great Waste and Profusion, but it was not in his Power to give him good Sense. That is the Gift of God and Nature alone, and is not to be taught; and *Greek* and *Latin*, without it, only cumber and overload a weak Head, and often render the Fool more abundantly foolish. I must therefore confess, that I have ever had, from my first Acquaintance with History, a most contemptible Opinion of this Monarch; which has perhaps been much heightened and increased, by my long studying and conning over the Materials of this History. For he appears, in his Dealings with the ⌜Virginia⌝ Company, to have acted with such mean Arts and Fraud, and such little Tricking, as highly misbecome Majesty."

Stith's education at Queen's College and his acquaintance with the best examples of English historical writing prepared him for a careful study of the history of Virginia, during which, as he tells us, he regarded "Truth as the first requisite and principal Virtue in an Historian, and relating nothing without a sufficient Warrant and Authority." He paid tribute to Captain John Smith's *Generall Historie*, but he found its materials confused. Among his other sources were the papers of his uncle, Sir John Randolph, and the records of the London Company, made available to him by William Byrd.

From its publication in 1747 to the present time, Stith's *History* has influenced subsequent writings and is considered a standard authority, although Stith was hampered by having only a few of the corporation records before 1618 and very few of the national official records of England. The book has had a great impact on the thinking regarding the frontier boundaries of Virginia, and it was quoted by Joshua Fry in his report in 1751 as one of the authorities for the map boundaries he drew.

The first part of the work depends heavily on Captain John Smith's *Generall Historie* and the later sections on the records of the London Company, and it was these records that convinced Stith that the London Company was far more concerned with the rights and the well-being of the Colonists than was King James I.

Stith's *History* not only demonstrated a growing native concern for America's past, seen also in Samuel Smith's *The History of the Colony of . . . New-Jersey* (1765) and in John Callender's *Historical Discourse on the . . . Colony of Rhode-Island* (1739), but it also appeared during a time when the prohibition against printing in the Province of Virginia was relaxed. The degree to which expression was at an early period controlled has been made familiar by the much-quoted utterance of Sir William Berkeley, royal Governor of Virginia, in his report to the Lords Commissioners of Foreign Plantations in 1671: "But, I thank God, *there are no free schools* nor *printing*, and I hope we shall not have these hundred years; for *learning* has brought disobedience, and heresy, and sects into the world, and *printing* has divulged them, and libels against the best government. God keep us from both!" In 1683 the King had ordered that in Virginia "no person be permitted to use any press for printing upon any occasion whatsoever," but in 1690 this was changed so that a press could be set up with the permission of the Governor.

Stith's printer, William Parks, who had a press in Ludlow, England, established himself in Williamsburg in 1730 to print the documents of the Virginia Assembly. In 1836 he began the *Virginia Gazette*, the first journal in the Colony, and eleven years later he issued Stith's *History*. Printing in Virginia was now well established and had some degree of freedom.

Stith's *History* ends with the dissolution of the London Company in 1624. He had intended to carry the work forward in several more volumes and to include many of his sources, but he found, to his surprise and mortification, that his countrymen "seemed to be much alarmed, and to grudge, that a complete History of their own Country would run to more than one Volume, and cost them above half a Pistole." His one volume remains the only scholarly history of Virginia up to his time and a valuable source.

RAY W. FRANTZ JR.
University Librarian,
University of Virginia

V

South Carolina

Charleston Library Society

*Rules of the Society for Erecting a Library,
and Raising a Fund for an Academy*

1750

RULES
OF THE
SOCIETY
For erecting a
LIBRARY,
And raising a FUND
FOR AN
ACADEMY
At *Charles-Town* in *South-Carolina*.

SOUTH-CAROLINA:
Charles-Town, Printed by *Peter Timothy*, 1750.

V. *South Carolina*

THE early Colonists of South Carolina were the first to appropriate public funds for the support of a library. In 1698 three hundred pounds sterling was raised to support the establishment of a library in Charleston. The effort, headed by the Rev. Thomas Bray, obtained thirty pounds from the Lords Proprietors of the Colony, and the Assembly paid the balance due (fifty-three pounds) on the books sent out in the original shipment of 1698. In 1700 laws were enacted concerning the use of the library. These were the first library laws passed in the Colonies.

The interest in libraries continued in South Carolina, but it was not until 1748—after the establishment of the Library Company of Philadelphia in 1731 and the Redwood Library at Newport, Rhode Island, in 1747—that the Charleston Library Society was actually founded. This library was a subscription, rather than a public, library. In that year seventeen men from varied walks of life (they included a printer and a wig-maker, as well as lawyers, planters, and merchants) joined together to make a modest investment of ten pounds in pamphlets. The Charleston Library Society grew from this slight beginning.

The members of the group realized the possibilities of expanding their society, and in 1750 Peter Timothy, one of the original seventeen members, published *Rules of the Society for Erecting a Library, and Raising a Fund for an Academy. . . .*

These rules expanded the institution from a small social body to an established subscription library, similar to those at Newport and Philadelphia. Provision was made for an initial expenditure of sixteen hundred pounds sterling (that is, British currency—rather than South Carolina's Colonial currency, which was worth only one-seventh of its British counterpart) for books. Thereafter a further one hundred pounds sterling was to be available each year for new purchases, such to be financed from a weekly membership subscription of five South Carolina shillings.

The subscription libraries of this era were an attempt to augment personal or private libraries, which were limited by the expense of importing books from Europe. Subscription libraries contained current pamphlets and periodicals, histories, religious books, medical and scientific works, works of general information, the Classics, and literature. But also, in keeping with the trend in the 18th Century, they emphasized books in the practical-aids and political fields.

The publication of the *Rules* of the Charleston Library Society typifies the strong activity underway throughout the American Colonies in establishing libraries and educational institutions, to serve as cultural centers. The inadequate schools of the day led to having most formal education center around library collections. Thus, the importance of books greatly affected the ability of the Colonists to train their children. The subscription libraries enhanced this ability.

The 18th-Century regulations for the operation of Charleston's Library Society are of considerable and striking interest. For example, the length of the loan period was based upon the distance the borrower lived from the library and also on the size of the book. Although provision was made for the election of a librarian on an annual basis, the position was evidently honorary.

Use of the Society's facilities was effectively restricted to the wealthier members of the community. The weekly membership fee of five shillings amounted to an annual rate of two pounds sterling, a considerable sum at that time. Moreover, unlike Franklin's Library Company of Philadelphia, to which any "civil gentleman" might be admitted (although only members might borrow books), the Charleston regulations stipulated that no one might be admitted to the library "before he has been proposed and approved as a Member" (Rule xxi). Clearly, despite the fact that the founders saw their library as performing not only a social recreational function, but also an educational one, they did not intend to make it available to other than individuals of their own class.

Among the most important and interesting of the intentions of the Society is that contained in its Rule XI. This provides for the interest from invested funds from subscriptions to be used to purchase "Instruments for a Course of experimental Philosophy." Additional interest was to be applied to establish professorships, firstly, in mathematics and natural and experimental philosophy and, later, in other subjects not specified at the time of the framing of the regulations.

The founders of the Charleston Library Society had two aims, the establishment of a subscription library and the creation of an institution of higher learning in South Carolina. Had their plan come to full fruition, as (presumably for financial reasons) it did not, the projected new academy would have been the first of its kind south of Williamsburg. As it was, the wealthy merchants and planters of South Carolina continued to send their sons to the North and to England for an education, or they employed private tutors, and education at a college level was not available within the State until the foundation of the College of Charleston (1785) and the South Carolina College at Columbia (1801).

The Society did flourish, however, in its role as a library. In 1755 the Colonial legislature granted a charter of incorporation. In the following year the Society had one hundred and sixty members, and by 1758 it was on a sound financial footing, numbering the most prominent figures of the community among its membership—and with the royal Governor of the Colony as its president.

The Society's library has continued to the present day and is a strong research library.

KENNETH E. TOOMBS
Director of Libraries,
University of South Carolina

VI

New Jersey

Issue Number 1

The New American Magazine

1758

THE NEW
Americaŋ Magazine:

Nº I. For January, 1758

CONTAINING,

I. The History of North-America, continued.
II. The Traveller, continued.
III. The Monthly Miscellany.

IV. Poetical Essays.
V. The Chronological Diary.
VI. The Historical Chronicle.
VII. Naval Engagements.

Magna est veritas, et prevalebit.

To be continued Monthly. Price, One Shilling, Proc.

[❦❦❦❦❦❦❦❦❦❦❦❦❦❦❦❦❦❦❦❦❦❦❦❦❦❦❦❦❦❦❦❦❦❦❦❦]

By Sylvanus Americanus.

❦❦❦❦❦❦❦❦❦❦❦❦ ❦❦❦[❦❦]❦❦❦❦❦❦❦❦❦❦❦❦❦❦❦

Woodbridge, in NEW-JEREY:

Printed and Sold by James Parker. Sold also by Parker and Weyman in New-York, and by Thomas Coombe, in Front-Street, Philadelphia

VI. *New Jersey*

ABSTRACT journals, digests, and journals of amusement were established in 17th-Century Great Britain, to be followed in the 18th Century by the essay periodical. The first magazine of the modern type, featuring a miscellany of information and opinion, was *The Gentleman's Magazine*, published from 1731 to 1907. Its chief rival was *The London Magazine; or, Gentleman's Monthly Intelligencer* (1732–1785), but it was only one of several. The magazine was slow to be successfully transplanted to America. Jeremy Belknap explained this to a prospective publisher who sought his advice: "Such country as this is not yet arrived at such a pass of improvement to keep up one or two monthly vehicles of importance."

A number of shaky ventures were, nevertheless, begun in the Colonies. Unfortunately, both low advertising and low circulation income were common. What advertising there was appeared, in most cases, only on the covers, in supplements, and on the final pages. The average price of a shilling a copy for the five hundred or so copies of each issue published was barely sufficient to keep a magazine solvent. Postal regulations were also restrictive—and sometimes subject to manipulation against competition by publishers who also served as postmasters.

The first magazines published in what is now the United States began in 1741, in Philadelphia, and in Boston in 1743. Several more soon followed, but none of the early efforts was both long-lived and of substantial content, until *The American Magazine, and Monthly Chronicle* was launched at Philadelphia in October of 1757. Its essays ranged beyond the topic of politics that predominated in the pages of its predecessors, and early issues included such varied articles as "The Philosophy of Earthquakes," "An Attempt to Account for the Luminous Appearance of the Sea in the Night-time," "Proposal for a Militia in Pennsylvania," "Character of the King of Prussia," "New Experiments in Electricity," and "On the Pernicious Use of Spiritous Liquors."

The New American Magazine of Woodbridge, New Jersey, began only a few months later, in January of 1758. It featured not only current events, but also essays, tales, and verse. Its editor, Judge Samuel Nevill (who was styled "Sylvanus Americanus" on the title page), had been editor of the London *Evening Post*. The magazine's ambitious publisher was James Parker, who enterprisingly arranged for its sale in New York, Philadelphia, and elsewhere throughout the Colonies.

The matter included was, as is evident from the table of contents, varied; and the initial volume was launched featuring monthly installments of a monographic work entitled *The History of North America*. Demand was apparently brisk from the outset, as the second number (February 1758) carried this notice: "A greater demand for this *Magazine*, than was expected, having taken off all the first Number since its publication; we would inform such as may be yet desirous of subscribing, that, if any number shall appear by the finishing our next, the first half-sheets of the history will be reprinted, in order to complete the books of such as are desirous of having them bound up, at the rate of 2d. for each half-sheet; or, if a large number of subscribers do desire it, the whole magazine shall be reprinted."

That, however, the publication was not considered, either by its editorial director or its readers, to have achieved instant perfection is suggested by comments published in December of 1758: "The first year of this Magazine being ended, the *Author* thinks himself obliged to look back on his work, and to consider how far he hath answer'd the *Readers* expectations, or his own engagements: And he finds great reason to think he hath failed in both. . . . One complaint from some of his readers is, that there are in it too many grave Essays, and that the composition is not enlivened with that polite wit and humour necessary to amuse as well as instruct: This the *Author* frankly confesses may be true. . . ."

However, the editor asserts, "As the *Author* by industry, and at a considerable expence, hath extended his correspondence, whereby he is now furnished with proper materials, he begs leave to assure his *Readers*, that his MAGAZINE shall be a *Conservatory* for those pieces of literature, wit, and useful knowledge, which deserve the general notice of mankind and which by being published in loose papers, would otherwise perish, or by being included in large and expensive volumes, are not easily to be obtained by common readers, or by being printed on political occasions, and for partial purposes, are out of the way of the generality of the common people."

The fate of *The New American Magazine* was no different from that of its ten predecessors, however; it ceased publication after only twenty-seven months. In the fourteen years that followed only three new magazines were launched, but one of them surviving more than nine months. Even the great interest in the subsequent War for Independence did not help the struggling industry; both the *Pennsylvania Magazine* and the *United States Magazine* failed.

A brief list of some of the contributors to early United States magazines illustrates that they were, nevertheless, perceived as institutions of considerable importance in educating the public: Washington, Franklin, Hamilton, Jay, Rush, Witherspoon, Paine, Freneau, Randolph, Hancock, Brackenridge, and Rittenhouse.

While nearly a hundred magazines were to appear by 1801, according to William Beer's *Checklist of American Magazines*, generally only one or two were being published at one time, until the 19th Century. By 1825, however, over one hundred were currently published, and by 1850 there were more than six hundred. By 1879 Congress recognized the importance of magazines and stimulated their distribution through the enactment of provision for them to enjoy low-cost mailing privileges.

RICHARD D. BOSS
University Librarian,
Princeton University

VII

Maryland

Abraham Milton

The Farmer's Companion

1761

THE

FARMER's
COMPANION,

DIRECTING

How to Survey Land

AFTER

A new and particular METHOD.

By ABRAHAM MILTON, Farmer,
of *Kent* County, in *Maryland*.

ANNAPOLIS: Printed for the AUTHOR.
MDCCLXI.

VII. *Maryland*

OF Abraham Milton little is known. Variously described as an "Inspector at Chestertown" and a "farmer of Kent County," his claim to bibliographic immortality rests upon his work entitled *The Farmer's Companion*, a 1761 treatise on surveying. The publication was, as is revealed by consulting Lawrence C. Wroth's bibliography of Maryland imprints through the year 1776, the first manual of its kind to be issued in Colonial Maryland. Indeed, it was probably the first in any of the Middle-Atlantic Colonies.

The earliest known example of the press in Maryland bears the date 1689. Wroth cites, in his historical account of printing within the Province, that the "first recorded evidence," on the other hand, "of the presence of a printer in Maryland occurs in an act of Assembly for October 1686." And this, he notes, would involve the following order for the establishment of presses in the American Colonies during the 17th Century: "Massachusetts, 1638; Virginia, 1682; Pennsylvania, 1685; Maryland, 1686; New York, 1693." (The other eight Colonies were not to experience the introduction of the printer's craft until the 18th Century, in this order: Connecticut, 1709; New Jersey and Rhode Island in the 1720s; South Carolina, 1731; North Carolina in 1749; New Hampshire, 1756; and, finally, Delaware and Georgia during the '60s.)

Pioneer printing in Maryland long gave primary attention, as was the case elsewhere among the Colonies, to the publication of the acts and the proceedings of the Provincial government. An occasional sermon or theological discourse, almanacs, newspapers, and advertisements comprised the remainder of the printed output of the Colony well into the 18th Century.

Little attention was given, early on in America, to works of a practical nature. True, instructional manuals, often in the form of primers and catechisms, constituted a widespread and constant element of Colonial printing, but treatises on the agricultural, the mechanical, and the domestic arts and sciences were late to appear. Perhaps such manuals were available from abroad; perhaps the skills which would therein be covered were more readily acquired through observation and emulation, rather than by means of the printed word.

The mid-1700s saw, however, a proliferation of pamphlets, privately published by gentlemen farmers, setting forth their convictions and speculations on agricultural and related matters. Abraham Milton's *Companion* is a notable example of this kind of work, presenting, as it does, his principles for surveying without a compass, for platting land, for gauging time and distance without the usual implements normally employed for such tasks.

Anxious to share his inventions, Milton advertised in the *Maryland Gazette* in 1759 his intent to issue his work by subscription, assuming that four hundred subscriptions, at twenty shillings each, were received. In the spring of the following year another advertisement appeared, this time introducing a sliding scale upon which the price of the volume would be based if five hundred or more subscribers came forward. August of 1760 saw yet another ad, in which Milton announced that he intended to proceed with publication, even though the required number of subscriptions had not been realized. Then, at last, on April 23, 1761, the *Maryland Gazette* carried a notice to the effect that the work had, indeed, that day been published, to be sold for "10s. Ready money only."

The pamphlet consists of thirty-four pages, plus an engraved folding plate of illustrations of geometric figures, inserted opposite the first page of the text. Quotation of its closing section will provide an indication of the nature and flavor of the matter covered in *The Farmer's Companion*: "I would advise the Farmer to beautify his Plantation with an Orchard, and to set the same in true Rows, which may be easily done; for on any Part intended for an Orchard, lay down a Square, which if he hath not one ready made, he may make on Paper; and having placed the same for the Beginning of the Orchard, then lay out a Thread, true on each Square Line, as far as Four Trees will reach, then measure by the Threads the true Distance each Tree is to be, the one from the other, and set down a straight Stick at the End of each Measure, and so by setting up Sticks in a true Square, you may plant your Trees in a regular Manner, and have them at the true Distance of those first Planted."

For many years but one copy of *The Farmer's Companion* was known to exist, and it was held in private hands. In 1935 that unique extant copy was acquired by the Maryland Historical Society where it now resides, a testament to the ingenuity (and the tenaciousness) of its author—and an example, as well, of the concerns of an era not so long past in the weight of years, but far distant when measured in terms of the sophistication in methods and techniques which has come to pass in the interim.

H. JOANNE HARRAR
Librarian,
University of Maryland

VIII

Delaware

Thomas Fox

The Wilmington Almanack
for the Year 1762

1761

The WILMINGTON

ALMANACK,

OR

EPHEMERIES,

FOR

The YEAR of our LORD, 1762:

1762

Being the Second after LEAP-YEAR.

(On an *exceeding good* OLD PLAN.)

CONTAINING

The Motions of the Sun and Moon; the true Places and Aspects of the Planets; the rising and setting of the Sun; and the rising, setting and southing of the Moon.

ALSO,

The Lunations, Conjunctions, Eclipses, Judgment of the Weather, rising and setting of the Planet, Length of Days and Nights, Fairs, Courts, Roads, Quakers General Meeting, &c. Together with useful Tables, chronological Observations, and entertaining Remarks, in Prose and Verse.

Fitted to the Latitude of Forty Degrees, and a Meridian of near Five Hours West from London; *but may, without sensible Error, serve all the* NORTHERN COLONIES.

By THOMAS FOX, Philom.

WILMINGTON,
Printed and Sold by JAMES ADAMS, in *Market-street:*
----And to be had, in *Philadelphia,* of WILLIAM FALKNER, the second House from the First Presbyterian Church, in *Market-street.*

VIII. *Delaware*

PRINTING came late to Delaware—the three lower counties of William Penn's proprietary colony designated "Pennsylvania and the Three Lower Counties." Although it had succeeded by 1704 in securing from Penn the right to its own legislature, total separation from Pennsylvania was not achieved until the creation, in 1776, of the Delaware State. Of the original thirteen Colonies, all but Georgia had a printing press when James Adams established Delaware's first press and bookshop at Wilmington in September of 1761. The closeness and easy accessibility of Philadelphia, then the largest city in English America, and the sparse, largely rural population of the "Three Lower Counties" were factors which must have discouraged printers looking for new fields to cultivate. In 1774 the population of the Colony was estimated at just over thirty-five thousand, and its largest city, Wilmington, even by 1800 had only 3,241 inhabitants.

James Adams was an Irishman who worked in the Philadelphia printing shop of Franklin and Hall for some seven years before establishing himself in Wilmington. It proved to be a wise move, and Adams prospered in his adopted state, where for the better part of twenty-five years his was the only printing office. Undoubtedly, the best-known of Adams's publications is John Filson's *The Discovery, Settlement and Present State of Kentucke* (1784). Adams's production was typical of that of the Colonial printers, including legal forms, compilations of laws, spelling books—and, of course, almanacs.

In early America almanacs were staple productions of, and a sure source of income for, the printer, and it is not surprising, particularly since Adams must have been intimately acquainted with the success of Benjamin Franklin's "Poor Richard," that one of his earliest works was *The Wilmington Almanack, or Ephemeries, for The Year of our Lord, 1762*, by Thomas Fox, Philom. (The identity—if he ever existed outside of Adams's imagination—of Fox is unknown.) Adams continued the publication of this almanac until his death, when it was carried on by his successors.

Almanacs were popular in Europe and England before America was settled, so the early publication of an American almanac was inevitable. Indeed, the first "book" published in the Colonies was Pierce's *Almanack Calculated for New England*, printed by Stephen Daye at Cambridge, Massachusetts, in 1639. The importance of the almanac to Colonial America would be difficult to overstate. It was practically indispensible to the Colonial farm and household. The Bible and the almanac were the books most often found in the Colonial home, and it has been estimated that during the 17th and 18th Centuries the number of almanacs published outnumbered all other books together. Drake's *Almanacs of the United States*, a bibliography of more than fourteen thousand, attests to the almanac's widespread vogue and longevity.

James Adams was no innovator, and the content of his almanac follows what had become an almost standard pattern: A figure of the "Man of Signs" (relating parts of the body to the signs of the Zodiac); the calendar, giving dates in both Old Style and New, with its tables of sunrise and sunset and the place of the sun in the heavens, as well as the rising and setting of the moon; and the column headed "Aspects," which gave the phases of the moon and other important information. There are mileage charts northeast to Boston and southeast to Charleston (both starting at Philadelphia!). Each issue carried an essay, a poem, or some other reading matter.

In the "Aspects" column Adams has followed Franklin's example and filled in the lines with proverbs, and gives moral advice in a section entitled "Excellent Rules and Observations." Alas, these are not so pithy nor so witty as Poor Richard's. Adams obviously hoped for sales beyond the small population of Wilmington and Delaware, for although his tables were calculated for 40° (the latitude of Philadelphia, but the closest parallel to Wilmington), he professes that they may "without sensible Error, serve all the Northern Colonies"; and he lists Quaker general meetings, fairs, and sessions of courts in Maryland, New Jersey, Pennsylvania, and New York, as well as in Delaware. Whether or not his *Wilmington Almanack* had a custom much beyond the borders of Delaware is a matter for conjecture, but its long life proves that it must have been financially successful.

Today, the best-known of the Colonial almanacs is, of course, Franklin's *Poor Richard's Almanack*, written with wit and wisdom by Franklin himself. Appearing first in 1733, it soon became one of the best-selling almanacs and was sold not only in Philadelphia, but as far away as Charleston and Boston.

Poor Richard's Almanack gave its readers the standard fare, but the difference lay in Franklin's proverbs and maxims, and in the humorous, satirical, teasing letters to the reader from Franklin's alter ego, Poor Richard Saunders (and his goodwife, Bridget). Little of this matter was truly original with Franklin. His fanciful prediction, for example, of the demise of his rival "almanacer," Titan Leeds, was a ploy borrowed from Swift's Bickerstaff papers, and the still-quoted aphorisms of Poor Richard were combed from a variety of authors and anthologies. But it was Franklin's genius to sharpen the proverbs and twist them to the American taste. Poor Richard's sayings were known in Europe, as well as in America, and were translated into several languages. Many have endured these two hundred and more years, and they are often repeated today—as, to Franklin's amusement, they were to *him* in England, France, and Colonial America.

JOHN M. DAWSON
Director of Libraries,
University of Delaware

IX

Georgia

Issue Number 1

The Georgia Gazette

1763

THE
GEORGIA GAZETTE.

NUMBER 1.   THURSDAY, APRIL 7, 1763.

EUROPEAN INTELLIGENCE.

Moscow, November 15.

THE Empress keeps her apartments, not through illness but precaution. The Count Woronzow has given a grand entertainment to the Earl of Buckinghamshire, to which all the foreign ministers were invited.

Vienna, Dec. 11. We daily expect the news of a general action between the Prince of Holberg and the Prussians in Franconia.

Hamburgh, Dec. 17. The Prussian irruption into Franconia makes a great noise. The princes of the empire once took a resolution to apply for succour to the French King as guarantee of the treaty of Westphalia, but this design was waved on their being informed that the French troops were in consequence of the preliminaries between England and that crown, to evacuate the empire so soon as the ratifications were exchanged, and to return no more during this war.

Hague, Dec. 21. We hear from Madrid, that the King of Spain has granted a pension of ten thousand livres to the widow of Don Velasco, who so bravely defended the Moro Fort at the Havanna; and has given his son a title of nobility in Castile, which he is to bear by the name of the Marquis of the Fort Moro. His Majesty has likewise given directions, that there should be always, for the future, one ship in the royal navy of the name of Velasco.

Paris, Dec. 27. The Duke of Bedford is preparing a grand equipage, in order to his public entry in quality of Embassador Extraordinary from his Britannick Majesty, which is to be made about the middle of February next. This ceremony will give an additional lustre to the festivals then to be celebrated on account of the conclusion of the peace; and, to augment the splendor of this solemnity, an equestrian statue of his present Majesty, already finished, is then to be erected.

LONDON, December 24.

Admiralty-Office, December 24.

VICE-Admiral Sir Charles Saunders gives an account, in his letter of the 9th of last month, from Gibraltar, that the day before arrived at that port, his Majesty's ship the Brune, commanded by Capt. Tonyn, with the Oiseau, a French frigate of 26 guns, and about 240 men, which he fell in with and took the 23d of October, about seven leagues N. W. by W. from Carthagena. The Brune had six men killed, and 14 wounded, in the engagement; and there were 49 killed and wounded on board the Oiseau. The Chevalier de Modene, her Captain, lost his right arm: Three of his officers are wounded, and all the rest of them killed. *London Gazette.*

Dec. 27. It is reported that the Earl of Grenville will soon resign his place of President of the Council on account of his great age and bad state of health, and that the Lord Chancellor is to resign the seals and succeed him in that important office, which will occasion a general promotion among the gentlemen of the law.

From Ratisbon they send us a rumour that the Ministers of England and Prussia have been ordered by the Grand Signior to quit Constantinople.

Letters by this day's mail advise, that a negotiation between the courts of Vienna and Berlin is in great forwardness.

We have also a report that the Count de Seilern is coming to England with the character of Minister Plenipotentiary from the Empress Queen to renew the good understanding between the two courts.

It is very strongly affirmed that the French have already sent ten men of war to the East-Indies, in order to be beforehand with us, and shew us some true French faith; and that a fleet of ours is already going there.

It is also affirmed that great obstacles to the definitive treaty have arisen, in consequence of some disputes between the French and English East-India companies.

Orders were sent on Thursday night to the War Office, to continue the light troops in full pay till the 23d of next month, not being yet ready to dismiss them.

Yesterday there was a cabinet council at St. James's on affairs relating to the army, at which Lord Ligonier and several officers of the army assisted.

We learn from Spain, that the money and effects of the Count de Superunda, late Viceroy of Peru, which had been landed at Ferrol from the Havanna, had been seized by the government, and the Count himself was expected to be put under arrest: That the money belonging to private persons returned from the Havanna had also been seized, because they had neglected to register it; but it was thought it would be restored.

Advices from Amsterdam pretend, that according to letters received there from Batavia, of the 6th of May, the English have received a considerable check on the coast of Coromandel, by the miscarriage of the attempt against the isle of France, and that, in an action at sea, we have also suffered a very great loss. Other letters from the same place bring accounts, that six of our vessels have been sunk near the isle of France; but it is hoped this will all prove Dutch news.

A gentleman from Portsmouth writes, that the French prisoners there express the utmost dissatisfaction on their being ordered home, and that great numbers of them, who were ordered on board for their return to France, had made their escape.

Last Friday the Buckingham militia was disembodied at Ailesbury, and had given them their regiment cloaths, knapsacks, &c. and each of them 14 days pay to carry them to their respective homes.

The Family Compact privateer of St. Sebastian's, of 10 guns and 100 men, is taken by the Boston frigate, Sir Thomas Adams, and brought into Plymouth.

The Calcutta Indiaman has actually brought home the last Frenchmen that remained on the whole continent of Asia; and Bencoolen, on the island of Sumatra, was retaken about 15 months ago by three of our Indiamen.—*Query, What conquests in the East-Indies has France to restore to England, in order to fulfil the 10th article of the preliminaries?*

By this ship we have also advice, that the forces destined for an expedition against the Manilla islands, were all ready to proceed, and only waited for an account of the declaration of war against Spain, and were in great expectations of success. But we have still a less pleasing account of the intended attack on the French at Mauritius, wisely planned by the late minister, for their utter extirpation from that quarter of the globe. Admiral Cornish, during his cruise and delay, in expectation of the promised succours from Europe, buried upwards of 1000 brave sailors, besides landmen, and returned sickly and distressed.

AMERICA.

Boston, October 18.

WE hear from Biddeford, in the county of York, that at the inferior court lately held there, a cause was tried between Thomas Hammet, of Berwick, in said county, yeoman, plaintiff, and Peter Staple, of Kittery, in the same county, gentleman, defendant, for the defendant's debauching the plaintiff's wife, &c. and after a full hearing of six hours, the jury brought in their verdict for the plaintiff to recover against the defendant 1000l. lawful money, damages and costs.

IX. *Georgia*

GEORGIA was the last of the thirteen American Colonies to be founded. It was created as a buffer to protect South Carolina from the Spanish in Florida and the French in Louisiana. Savannah was first settled in 1733, under the direction of James Edward Oglethorpe, and with a charter granted to the trustees in 1732. Georgia was one of the Colonies most remote from the principal centers of Colonial life, both political and economic.

The charter of Georgia's trustees expired in 1753, and it became a royal Province. Between 1753 and 1762 the new Province existed with no capability for distributing its acts, regulations, and news, other than by means of access to a printer in South Carolina. On March 4, 1762, Governor James Wright approved an act which made provisions for printing the laws of the Province and for encouraging a printer to set up a printing press. Up to that time it had been difficult to put laws into execution, and the intentions of the General Assembly and the Governor were often frustrated due to the inability to print and distribute the laws.

Probably another reason for the enactment of the new law was the fact that a printer by the name of James Johnston had recently arrived in the new Colony from England. He offered to set up a press if he received financial support to help him defray the expenses of equipping an office. Therefore, it was enacted that "the publick treasurer shall yearly and every year, pay unto the said James Johnston, or his heirs or assigns, the full sum of one hundred pounds . . . and that the said annual sum of one hundred pounds, granted and to be paid as aforesaid, to the said James Johnston, or his heirs or assigns, shall arise and be paid out of the general tax."

The first product of Johnston's press was *The Georgia Gazette*, issue "Number 1" of which appeared on April 7, 1763. This initial publication was unusual because the newspaper was, in fact, an arm of the state, meant to inform the populace about the laws and decisions of the governing authorities. In addition, the paper provided the commercial and political interests of the Colony with an organ which supplied information about happenings elsewhere.

It was a surprisingly informative newspaper, considering that each issue consisted of only four or six pages. In the paper's two main sections, headed "European Intelligence" and "America," it covered many happenings very thoroughly, including appointments by the English and the Colonial governing officials. In addition, there were advertisements and notices, many of which concerned runaway slaves. (For example, one ad in the first number seeks, "A tall Negroe Wench named Jeanie, this country born, and speaks good English. Whoever delivers said Wench to me," its subscriber declares, "shall have ten shillings reward." And another runaway is identified as, "A Negroe man, named *Primus*, belonging to James Skirving, Esq; of Ponpon." Again, a reward was offered.)

James Johnston, as was true of many Colonial printers, also ran a bookstore, and judging by the advertisement in the *Gazette*, of its wares, it is obvious that the Colony's population was not only enlightened, but intellectually well fed for the time, having access to reading materials which were of the best. Included in Johnston's book stocks were works by Swift, Defoe, Rollins, Hume, Addison, Congreve, Bacon, Dryden, Shakespeare, Butler, Locke, Pope, Young, Pascal, Molière, and Voltaire, in addition to many of the Classic authors.

By the year 1773, James Johnston was receiving the rather considerable sum of one hundred and eighty pounds, four shillings, and nine pence as compensation for his publication duties, which included issuance of *The Georgia Gazette*. The continuing payments which he received from the Colony, along with the other income he must have received as a printer-publisher-bookseller, demonstrate that Mr. Johnston was a rather wealthy man. As such, it would also be obvious that he was probably quite faithful to the Colonial officials, and a Loyalist.

The Georgia Gazette was published continuously from its founding to February 7, 1776—except for an interruption from November 21, 1765, until May 21, 1766. The interruption occurred because Johnston announced that he could not continue the *Gazette* as a publication if he could not make use of unstamped paper. With the repeal of the Stamp Act, publication of the *Gazette* resumed.

In late 1775, with the deterioration of the royal government, a Council of Safety was organized. At a meeting of the Council on January 16, 1776, a motion was made, seconded, and agreed to: "that a committee be appointed to examine the printer's office, to see whether there was not something to be published this week, that might endanger the public safety." On February seventh the last issue of *The Georgia Gazette* appeared, only three weeks after the Council's action. After the cessation of the publication of *The Georgia Gazette*, there was no publication or printing in Georgia for about a year.

The Georgia Gazette, therefore, represents a milestone in the history of Georgia. Not only is it Georgia's first printed publication, but in addition, the *Gazette* demonstrated that the governing authorities were enlightened enough to try bringing information to the populace at large.

WARREN N. BOES
Director of Libraries,
University of Georgia

X

Connecticut

John Trumbull

*An Essay on the Use and Advantages
of the Fine Arts*

1770

AN ESSAY

ON THE

USE AND ADVANTAGES

OF THE

FINE ARTS.

DELIVERED AT THE

PUBLIC COMMENCEMENT,

IN NEW-HAVEN,

SEPTEMBER 12TH. 1770.

by John Trumbull

NEW-HAVEN:

PRINTED BY T. AND S. GREEN.

also be obvious that he was probably quite faithful to the Colonial officials, and a Loyalist.

The Georgia Gazette was published continuously from its founding to February 7, 1776—except for an interruption from November 21, 1765, until May 21, 1766. The interruption occurred because Johnston announced that he could not continue the *Gazette* as a publication if he could not make use of unstamped paper. With the repeal of the Stamp Act, publication of the *Gazette* resumed.

In late 1775, with the deterioration of the royal government, a Council of Safety was organized. At a meeting of the Council on January 16, 1776, a motion was made, seconded, and agreed to: "that a committee be appointed to examine the printer's office, to see whether there was not something to be published this week, that might endanger the public safety." On February seventh the last issue of *The Georgia Gazette* appeared, only three weeks after the Council's action. After the cessation of the publication of *The Georgia Gazette*, there was no publication or printing in Georgia for about a year.

The Georgia Gazette, therefore, represents a milestone in the history of Georgia. Not only is it Georgia's first printed publication, but in addition, the *Gazette* demonstrated that the governing authorities were enlightened enough to try bringing information to the populace at large.

WARREN N. BOES
Director of Libraries,
University of Georgia

X

Connecticut

John Trumbull

*An Essay on the Use and Advantages
of the Fine Arts*

1770

AN ESSAY

ON THE

USE AND ADVANTAGES

OF THE

FINE ARTS.

DELIVERED AT THE

PUBLIC COMMENCEMENT,

IN NEW-HAVEN,

SEPTEMBER 12TH. 1770.

by John Trumbull

NEW-HAVEN:

PRINTED BY T. AND S. GREEN.

tures, friends, and both past and potential supporters throughout the Colonies. He defied his enemies (largely unidentified), and he promised never to be distracted from his central purpose. He described in detail his efforts to obtain Indian pupils for his School, and his attempts at "gospelizing" them, all against the most trying obstacles.

Pertinent to Wheelock's move to New Hampshire, the *Narrative* opens a view on the difficulties of educational development in an American wilderness setting: "I have found, and I think it reasonable to be expected in such an affair, and especially one so large as this, which I have been concern'd in, many necessities which were so contingent, that it was beyond the penetration or prudence of man to foresee, or provide against, wherein the expence of time, travel &c. to supply them, has been many fold more than the cost of the thing to be done, if it could have been affected with no greater difficulty than in ordinary cases in populous towns."

Finally, in listing his needs Eleazar Wheelock expressed the earnest hope that his "imperfect narrative may fall into the hands of such as God has honoured with an affluence of worldly goods . . . who may . . . be perswaded that this is a way acceptable and well pleasing to God, for them in return to honor him with their substance." Though the nature of the appeal has been altered in a more skeptical 20th Century, the tactic of all present-day private educational institutions may be said to have remained unchanged.

RICHARD W. MORIN
Librarian Emeritus,
Dartmouth College

XII

North Carolina

James Davis

The Office and Authority
of a Justice of Peace

1774

THE
Office and Authority
OF A
JUSTICE of PEACE.
AND ALSO,

The Duty of SHERIFFS, CORONERS, CON-
STABLES, CHURCHWARDENS, OVERSEERS
of ROADS, and other Officers.

TOGETHER WITH

PRECEDENTS of WARRANTS, JUDGMENTS, EXECU-
TIONS, and other legal PROCESS, iſſuable by Ma-
giſtrates within their ſeveral Juriſdictions, in Caſes
Civil and Criminal, with the Method of Judicial
Proceedings before Juſtices of the Peace out of Seſſi-
ons. Alſo ſome Directions for their Conduct within
their County Courts.

To which is added,

An APPENDIX.

Containing many uſeful PRECEDENTS, and Directions
for the Execution of them.

Collected from the Common and Statute Laws of
England, and the Acts of Aſſembly of this Province,
and adapted to our Conſtitution and Practice.

By *J. DAVIS*, Eſq; one of his Majeſty's Juſtices of
the Peace for the County of *Craven*.

NEWBERN:
Printed by JAMES DAVIS. M,DCC,LXXIV.

tures, friends, and both past and potential supporters throughout the Colonies. He defied his enemies (largely unidentified), and he promised never to be distracted from his central purpose. He described in detail his efforts to obtain Indian pupils for his School, and his attempts at "gospelizing" them, all against the most trying obstacles.

Pertinent to Wheelock's move to New Hampshire, the *Narrative* opens a view on the difficulties of educational development in an American wilderness setting: "I have found, and I think it reasonable to be expected in such an affair, and especially one so large as this, which I have been concern'd in, many necessities which were so contingent, that it was beyond the penetration or prudence of man to foresee, or provide against, wherein the expence of time, travel &c. to supply them, has been many fold more than the cost of the thing to be done, if it could have been affected with no greater difficulty than in ordinary cases in populous towns."

Finally, in listing his needs Eleazar Wheelock expressed the earnest hope that his "imperfect narrative may fall into the hands of such as God has honoured with an affluence of worldly goods . . . who may . . . be perswaded that this is a way acceptable and well pleasing to God, for them in return to honor him with their substance." Though the nature of the appeal has been altered in a more skeptical 20th Century, the tactic of all present-day private educational institutions may be said to have remained unchanged.

RICHARD W. MORIN
Librarian Emeritus,
Dartmouth College

XII

North Carolina

James Davis

The Office and Authority
of a Justice of Peace

1774

THE
Office and Authority
OF A
JUSTICE of PEACE.
AND ALSO,

The Duty of SHERIFFS, CORONERS, CON-
STABLES, CHURCHWARDENS, OVERSEERS
of ROADS, and other Officers.

TOGETHER WITH

PRECEDENTS of WARRANTS, JUDGMENTS, EXECU-
TIONS, and other legal PROCESS, iffuable by Ma-
giftrates within their feveral Jurifdictions, in Cafes
Civil and Criminal, with the Method of Judicial
Proceedings before Juftices of the Peace out of Seffi-
ons. Alfo fome Directions for their Conduct within
their County Courts.

To which is added,

An APPENDIX.

Containing many ufeful PRECEDENTS, and Directions
for the Execution of them.

Collected from the Common and Statute Laws of
England, and the Acts of Affembly of this Province,
and adapted to our Conftitution and Practice.

By *J. DAVIS*, Efq; one of his Majefty's Juftices of
the Peace for the County of *Craven.*

NEWBERN:
Printed by JAMES DAVIS. M,DCC,LXXIV.

XII. *North Carolina*

WHEN James Davis of New Bern published *The Office and Authority of a Justice of Peace* in 1774, he was sustaining in remote North Carolina a tradition which had begun in Medieval Europe. During the 16th and 17th Centuries varied editions of this kind of handbook appeared in increasing numbers, containing procedures, forms, and significant legal precedents. In the 18th Century, Colonial presses began to issue it, with appropriate adaptations to its new surroundings, to the undoubted benefit of untrained magistrates and lawyers. The pervasive spread of this "useful *vade mecum*," as Lawrence Wroth calls it, enabled the Colonists to maintain strong ties with their English heritage, for each successive printer repeated the citations of English common and statutory law made by his predecessors on major legal topics, before adding the pertinent law of his own Colony.

This unbroken chain of legal tradition is well demonstrated in Davis's book. In his preface, he refers to a book of the same title by George Webb, printed in Williamsburg in 1736 by the celebrated Virginia printer, William Parks. Originally, Parks had come from England, in 1725, to assume the office of public printer to the Province of Maryland, but five years later had moved to Williamsburg as public printer to Virginia. While there is little evidence on Davis's early life, it is known that he worked with Parks in Williamsburg. He probably learned his art from this master, and he undoubtedly had become familiar with Webb's book while working at the Williamsburg press.

Davis came to North Carolina in response to an invitation from the General Assembly to become the Colony's first public printer. He began his contract in June 1749, and three months later he produced his first imprint, *The Journal of the House of Burgesses*. Two years later, he issued *A Collection of All the Public Acts of Assembly, of the Province of North-Carolina: Now in Force and Use*. The printing of this compilation was clearly an excellent preparation for his later book, but Davis significantly augmented that preparation by entering the public life of the Colony. His periodically tumultuous career as public printer and as publisher of a series of short-lived newspapers apparently left him sufficiently free to serve for twenty-five years on the county court and for six in the General Assembly. More significantly, he received five appointments as a justice of the peace of Craven County. This experience, combined with his exposure to George Webb's book, provided him with an excellent background for the publication of his own—and North Carolina's —version of the traditional handbook.

For some fifteen years Davis had a monopoly of printing in North Carolina, the next-to-last Colony to have a printing press. Despite his isolation, Davis, both as a newspaper publisher and as printer of *The Office and Authority of a Justice of Peace*, was in the mainstream of Colonial printing and proved to be a worthy successor to Parks. The quality of his work, clearly evident in this book, was invariably of a high order.

The book is alphabetically arranged by legal issue, with appropriate case precedents and official forms appended. The past cases which Davis cited provide an interesting array of human folly and tragedy. For example, under the heading "Misdemeanor," he recounted the following tragicomic episode: "A Man and his Wife disagreeing, she applied herself to one *Golding*, a Parson, and offered him 40s. to whip her Husband: The Parson undertook it, and came in Woman's Cloaths to the Chamber where the Husband was, and endeavoured to whip him with a Rod; in striving they were both hurt. The Parson run away from the Husband, who died in a little Time after this Scuffle. All this being proved, the Wife and Parson were fined 500l. each."

The substance of the book, however, lies in the authoritative exposition of the English legal tradition, as seen in the following discussion of the limits imposed on search warrants: "Again, Lord *Hale*, in his History of the Pleas of the Crown, expresseth himself thus: I do take it, that a General Warrant to search in all suspected Places is not good; but only to search in such particular Places where the Party assigns before the Justice his Suspicion, and the probable Cause thereof; for these Warrants are judicial Acts, and must be granted upon Examination of the Fact."

It is difficult to imagine how Davis and his fellow printers in the Colonies could have better served their frontier communities, struggling to establish lasting institutions and the rule of law, than by bringing to them the rich legal heritage of Britain in this compact and practical form.

JAMES F. GOVAN
University Librarian,
University of North Carolina

XIII

Pennsylvania

Thomas Paine

Common Sense

1776

COMMON SENSE;

ADDRESSED TO THE

INHABITANTS

OF

AMERICA,

On the following interesting

SUBJECTS. *By Thomas Paine*

I. Of the Origin and Design of Government in general, with concise Remarks on the English Constitution.

II. Of Monarchy and Hereditary Succession.

III. Thoughts on the present State of American Affairs.

IV. Of the present Ability of America, with some miscellaneous Reflections.

Man knows no Master save creating HEAVEN,
Or those whom choice and common good ordain.
THOMSON.

PHILADELPHIA;
Printed, and Sold, by R. BELL, in Third-Street.
MDCCLXXVI.

XIII. *Pennsylvania*

REFLECTING on the events and feelings which had, nearly three years before, led to the issuance of his *Common Sense*, a pamphlet central to the Revolutionary movement that led to the end of America's Colonial era, Thomas Paine wrote in November of 1778:

"It was my fate to come to America a few months before the breaking out of hostilities. I found the disposition of the people such, that they might have been led by a thread and governed by a reed. Their suspicion was quick and penetrating, but their attachment to Britain was obstinate, and it was, at that time, a kind of treason to speak against it. They disliked the Ministry, but they esteemed the nation. Their ideas of grievance operated without resentment, and their single object was reconciliation. Bad as I believed the Ministry to be, I never conceived them capable of a measure so rash and wicked as the commencing of hostilities; much less did I imagine the nation would encourage it. I viewed the dispute as a kind of law-suit, in which I supposed the parties would find a way either to decide or settle it.

"I had," he continued, "no thoughts of independence or of arms. The world could not then have persuaded me that I should be either a soldier or an author. If I had any talents for either they were buried in me, and might ever have continued so. . . . But when the country, into which I had but just put my foot, was set on fire about my ears it was time to stir. It was time for every man to stir."

Paine was born in the English town of Thetford in 1737, the son of an impoverished corset-maker. He attended grammar school (his sole formal education) until the age of thirteen, when he was apprenticed to his father's trade. At age nineteen he was briefly in service as a privateer aboard the *King of Prussia*, and during the ensuing seventeen years he was, successively, corset-maker, exciseman, schoolteacher, exciseman (again), tobacconist, and grocer.

In 1774 he met and particularly impressed Benjamin Franklin. Shortly thereafter he sailed for Philadelphia, with Franklin's letters of introduction and recommendation, arriving in November. Pennsylvania's principal city readily provided stimulus to Paine's active mind. The lively mix—religious, ethnic, political, and economic—of its society encouraged ideas and debate, and Philadelphia was also rivaling Boston as the heart of the Colonial printing industry. (It was here, of course, beginning a half-century earlier, that Franklin himself had amassed a considerable fortune as a printer.)

Paine's masterful treatise, *Common Sense*, appeared on the tenth of January 1776. His chosen vehicle was the pamphlet—a dominant means, then flourishing within the printing centers in Colonial America, of disseminating opinion and argument and contention (this in extension of a centuries-old tradition which reached back to Europe). Pamphlets were cheap and quick to print and distribute, allowing for swift and timely response to the events and judgments of the moment.

As was often the case in "pamphleteering," Paine's *Common Sense* was published anonymously. Its author, in fact, went to great lengths to conceal his identity, even from his printer. The pamphlet's message immediately struck a responsive chord with a populace which had up until this point no general, unified position on the matters to which it related. It was an instantaneous success, selling over one hundred thousand copies in three months' time. (The entire population of the Colonies was then only about two million.) It is, indeed, still in print.

Paine argued for what had previously been hotly debated, but nowhere yet so popularly urged, the actual political separation of Britain and her American Colonies. (In fact, the "war" had already been underway for some ten months, since the commencement of hostilities at Lexington and Concord in Massachusetts; but most parties still looked forward hopefully to eventual conciliation and accommodation with His Majesty's government.) Importantly, *Common Sense* was written for and directed at the common man. Its arguments and language were direct and simple, but powerful; and Paine strictly avoided the convoluted reasoning characteristic of so many of his contemporary publicists.

Common Sense stirred controversy from the moment of its publication, and it continues to do so today (especially with regard to the true influence it and its separatist message may or may not have had on the history of American progression from largely self-governed Colonies to a politically independent nation). It is clear that at the time of its original issuance the publication stimulated—indeed, provoked—widespread and energetic public debate, for and against the idea of actual independence from Britain. (George Washington, it may be noted, in a letter written at the end of January 1776, cited approvingly "the sound doctrine and unanswerable reasoning contained in the pamphlet *Common Sense*.") It was highly significant in that fateful discussion and debate, throughout the Colonies, which culminated six months later in the drafting and signing of America's Declaration of Independence.

The weight of historical opinion appears inclined toward an assessment of Tom Paine as an excellent and successful propagandist, but one of limited capacity as a political theorist. But whether *Common Sense* originated, developed, or simply popularized an idea, there is no question of the publication's importance as a seminal document of that transitional phase of our history, the American Revolution, which carried Britain's thirteen American Colonies to nationhood, as the United States of America.

RICHARD DE GENNARO
Director of Libraries,
University of Pennsylvania

Acknowledgments

Gratitude is expressed to the institutions that have generously made available copies of the items featured in this selection of *Thirteen Colonial Americana*, as cited below, in order that facsimiles of their title pages might be included herein. (All reproductions are original size, except Items II, III, and IX, which appear in sixteen-percent reduction.) Special thanks are also tendered the officials of those libraries and societies, for their facilitating arrangements. Particular obligation is owed to Claire B. Packard, Virginia L. Close, and Stanley W. Brown, as well as to others of the staff of the Dartmouth College Library, for assistance accorded the Editor in connection with this volume's preparation.

I. Harvard College Library

II. Brown University Library

III. Library Company of Philadelphia

IV. College of William & Mary Library

V. Library of Congress

VI. New-York Historical Society

VII. Maryland Historical Society

VIII. Historical Society of Pennsylvania

IX. Massachusetts Historical Society

X. Yale University Library

XI. Dartmouth College Library

XII. University of North Carolina Library

XIII. Yale University Library

1000 copies
have been printed at
The Stinehour Press

haec olim meminisse
juvabit